SOLILOQUY TO THE NIGHT SKY

SOLILOQUY TO THE NIGHT SKY

by

Kathleen Gregg

Accents Publishing • Lexington, Kentucky • 2026

Printed in the United States of America

Accents Publishing
Editor: Katerina Stoykova
Cover Image: *Layers 1* by Marta Dorton

Library of Congress Control Number: 2026935571
ISBN: 978-1-961127-23-4
First Edition

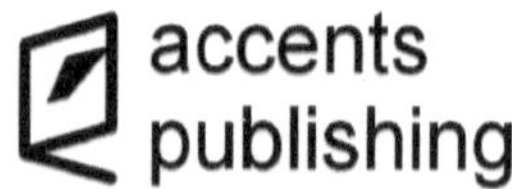

Accents Publishing is an independent press for brilliant voices. For a catalog of current and upcoming titles, please visit us on the Web at

www.accents-publishing.com

CONTENTS

For Wendy and Bird

NO OFF RAMP

windshield sky
is rain-heavy gray smeared
to the horizon   I'm going 80 mph
passing trucks on I-64
my sister

is on speaker phone
sobbing and
sobbing and
begging for her life
to make sense   again
and

     I can't help her

because   it never will   and

relentless traffic
is the only thing keeping me grounded
from the jolt
of my sister's distress   and

lightning lashes out
from the dark heart of the storm
as her voice cracks
I feel like I left and never came back

just enough awareness
to split us both down the middle

NANCY IS NEVER THE SAME

After her year of breast cancer therapy,
she knows it. *Chemo Brain is real.*
I'm not as sharp as I used to be. Still,
we believe surely, with time,
her fogginess will clear up. Surely.

Then, for the first time ever, she forgets
my birthday. No card, no phone call.
I let it go.

She tells me her *stupid* computer
won't let her open or print
my poems. Would I mind
mailing them instead? Of course.

She returns to the Apple Store
several times, certain her new
cell phone is faulty. Can't
get it to work right. Each time,
a salesperson shows her how
to use it. *They go too fast.*

Yes, they do.

NANCY CALLS ME, CRYING

Would I be too upset if she and Ed didn't
come this weekend? She just can't face
the long drive from Peoria.

*The trip is supposed to be fun, not stress
you out. It's okay. Of course, I won't love
you anymore, but no big deal.*

We both laugh. I've succeeded
in lifting her spirits. Jokes always work.

We'll come visit you. Soon.

Her relief floats between us. So does
her fragility.

I IGNORE THE SIGNS

my sister needs a dress
for her granddaughter's wedding
tells me she dreads the search
(my cue to offer help)
I jump at the chance
to do such a girl thing with her

she drives
complains about traffic
how far away the shopping center is
(we're there in fifteen minutes)
I spot a *Marshalls*
suggest we try there
my sister is surprised
says she's never heard of this store
I'm pretty certain the two of us
have shopped here before

once inside
my sister seems overwhelmed
not sure where to start
so I take the lead
pull dresses off the rack
she says *okay* to each one
I drape five or six
into the cart and make our way
toward the dressing rooms

I help her in and out of each choice
laughing when a dress is too tight
and I have to tug it off
none are flattering
she looks defeated

another round of browsing the racks
three more possibilities
back to the dressing room
I wiggle her into a navy-blue sheath
with bell sleeves
she looks in the mirror

draws in her breath
eyes radiant
this is the one
especially when she reads
the price tag
asks me
what's the name of this store again

she appears confused
when we walk out the door
and encounter the parking lot
would you like me to drive
she exhales a *yes*

on the way home
truth whispers
what I don't want to hear
my sister could not have found
a dress on her own

my heart pleads *shut up*
she's just having a bad day

ODE TO MY SISTER

storyteller   prankster
Rock of Gibraltar in my life
my stand-in mom
smart ascending feminist
she will never know
how many times
her unfaltering acceptance grabbed
my hands and hauled me
up from the cliff

even from a distance
I heard her smile
felt her eyes say
it's okay   I'm here   I'll always be here

in the throes of dementia
she still hugs me close
pats my back while
I inhabit her world
of fading memories
meet her in each moment

THE END OF PRETENDING

I feel Nancy hunt and hunt for words,
as if she is riffling through a box of loose photos.

Mostly she just gives up, spits out a laugh,
Well it's gone. I try to make light of it, fill in

the blanks, fall back on our inside jokes. That lifeline
is fraying (face it) from the weight of my furious grip.

Today, I attempt to reminisce about our cousins,
the big family gatherings. Her flat voice admits,

I don't know who they are. And I hear
the first goodbye.

PLAYING IN THE BASEMENT

It takes two of us to pump the treadle
on the dusty, old player piano
      down in my Aunt Juanita's basement.
It takes the alternating down strokes
      of two sets of legs
to activate the pumps, valves, pneumatics
of this magical mechanical piano.

Five girl cousins push for the pedal-pumping seat.
The two oldest win: my sister and Linda,
      still a child at fifteen.
The rest of us pick out music rolls, dotted
with their tiny perforations, from the many
crammed into a musty cardboard box.
      We prop up the companion song book, sing
the familiar lyrics; our parents' music,
heard at home:

Oh, What a Beautiful Mornin'
Bicycle Built for Two
Sentimental Journey
I Ain't Got Nobody

The piano's sound is tinny; the bellows add
a slight whoosh. Our voices expand in clear, true tones.
And for a brief time,
      down in my Aunt Juanita's basement,
there are no wrong notes.

STORYTELLER

Five young neighbor girls sit
in a semi-circle, facing
my sister. The grass is soft
and cool under our maple tree.
We stay so still, we could be
posing for a photo or an artist's
rendering. But that's not it.

Nancy has conjured up
a magical world, just for us.
One giant tarantula, gold key
positioned on its back, guards
the treasure chest hidden
at the bottom of an abandoned
well. The black, hairy spider
with glowing yellow eyes peers
up at us and screeches. Five
little girls leap to their feet,
scream with terrified delight.

A perfect moment to leave us
hanging. Nancy promises to finish
tomorrow, hints at a fairy princess,
monarch butterflies, poppy dust.

NANCY AND I ARE WALKING THE PERIMETER

of Lutheran Hillside Village, in Peoria.
Nancy's voice seethes,

> *Ed never asked me if I wanted*
> *to move here. He made*
> *all the arrangements*
> *without me. I hate eating*
> *with a bunch of strangers.*
> *The apartment is so ugly*
> *and cramped. I'm living*
> *in a box.*

On the contrary, light spills
into the living space
from a wall of windows
overlooking the central courtyard.

> *Ed never talks to me*
> *anymore. I don't think*
> *he loves me. You know,*
> *he's having sex with several*
> *women. I've seen him*
> *leaving with them.*

This accusation stops me
in my tracks. I stifle a laugh
when I realize she is serious.
This distrust is completely
out of character, a rip
in her soft silk lining.

> I am adamant, *Ed would never*
> *do that.* She is just as certain,
> *Oh yes, he would. He wants*
> *to get rid of me.*

In that moment,
I hurt as much as she does.

GROUNDHOG DAY (2014)

My sister chooses to spend / her seventieth birthday / in Kentucky, with me and Charlie / I bake a four-layer cake / vanilla with vanilla buttercream frosting / our favorite / we sing Happy Birthday off-key / family joke / always good for laughs / she tears up / opening my gift of pearls

next day brings snow / Nancy and I pull on / Charlie's old ski suits / stomp around in the snow / plop on the ground / make snow angels / giggle as we struggle to stand / like we did as kids / bright white / splash of cold / my sister's beautiful exuberance / joy earmarks / what becomes her last visit

BORDER LINE

Sometimes I imagine my sister
as an exile, relocated
to a desolate landscape, forced
to wander along unfamiliar paths
and scrubby terrain inhabited
by filmy shapes she can't quite
define. Home is no longer

her beacon, a hunger. Home
lies beyond the foggy horizon,
sunken, irretrievable.

I have been traveling through
Nancy's changing consciousness
for years; the same pilgrimage I took
with our mother before she died.

Lately, I imagine I lose
my own compass, stumble
into those same dark regions,
forget my way home.

A FIVE-MINUTE PHONE CONVERSATION WITH MY SISTER

Nancy has forgotten how to use her cell phone.
She only fumbles with it, confused and helpless.
Her husband, Ed, is my intermediary today.

Since he and Nancy live in the same retirement
village, it's a short walk from his apartment
to her memory care unit. He makes this trip
every day.

At the designated time, I call Ed's cell. He hands
the phone to Nancy, reminds her to hold it to her ear.
I sing *Happy Birthday* in an off-key, falsetto voice.
She laughs, has a vague notion who I am, but no idea
what day it is. I tell her not to eat too much cake.

A few years ago, she might have joked, *I'll eat
the whole damn cake if I want to.* My cue to say,
I'm gonna tell mom. Silly sister stuff. Maybe
she is trying to kid with me. But her words
are garbled, make no sense. I tell her I love her.

Ed prompts her to say goodbye. She struggles
to answer, *Okay.* The space between us is like
standing in a cave, hearing the last echoes.

WHAT A DIFFERENCE THE RIGHT MEDS MAKE

I discover my sister chatting
with two nurses, her arms folded
over a table, relaxed. She smiles,
recognizes me and her two
daughters, declares *It's Bird!*
which floors us. She hasn't
remembered that nickname
in months. The nurses laugh, say

Meet the new Nancy. Wait
till you see her dance!

A few words of encouragement,
"Mustang Sally" cranked up
on the nurse's iPad, and my sister
starts to sway, swing her arms
to the right, to the left. All of us
join in, like backup singers, joy
bubbling out of our mouths.

Last notes fade. We clap, cheer,
grin at each other in wonderment
and overwhelming relief and
with a sense of the old playfulness
we thought was gone forever.

I realize my sister is still confused,
her memories jumbled, disappearing.
But her terror, my helplessness
in the face of it, has been lowered
to the bottom of the well.

SIGHTINGS

A glee club of honks draws
my eyes skyward. Canada geese
soar
across beaming blue sky,
a rippling chevron
of sound and wing,
                    life in full flight.
Like my sister,

once. Not this ghost of a feather
detached, adrift
in thickening fog. Life
about to lose
            visibility.

I watch the formation shrink
to a black arrow shooting
south. Most geese will survive
this grueling migration, never question
their fate.
          They just fly.

And I am pierced by that truth,
and by this: is improbable joy found
in the float
from one awareness into another?
How can I ever know?
I simply keep my eyes
strained
for that last precious
              glimpse.

NO FALSE HOPE

When I visit now, I am faced
with a body emptied of you.

Your heart still beats its rhythm,
lungs push air in and out.

If a nurse lifts a spoon to your lips,
you open, chew and swallow.

Sometimes, the aides park you
in front of the common room TV.

You stare at the screen with eyes
devoid of awareness. This is

how I find you today. I squat
in front of your wheelchair, smile,

say *Hi, Nancy, it's me, your sister,*
and you turn those blank eyes on me.

I don't expect recognition anymore.
But I long for you, long

for you to be surviving
in an alternate state,

where the touch of my hand,
the stories I try to amuse you with,

the love streaming out from me,
still reach you.

LOST IN A MEMORY CARE UNIT

1.

I glimpse my sister shuffling down
the wide, carpeted hallway, sweater
wrapped tight, her arms hugged
around her midriff.
Catching up to her, I see no
recognition brighten her eyes. I pull
my mask away from my face.
It's me. Your baby sister!

She gasps, stares at me.
How are you here?

We hug, and she cries softly.
I circle my arm around this frail
version of my sister. *Let's walk.*
She smiles, *Okay.* Then I notice
her stained pants are inside out
and backwards.

2.

I'd really like to see my sister,
my sister tells me, as we sit
side-by-side on her unmade bed.
I take my mask off.
It's me, Nancy! I'm here!
Her eyes search my face. I see
a glimmer.

3.

*Remember how we used to sing
off-key, on purpose, while we did
the dishes at night until mom*

would finally yell, Oh for god's
sake, shut up!

Yes! Her head is bobbing.
We laugh, and for a second,
light shines from her eyes.

4.

We are looking at a few framed
photos someone has placed
on her bedside table. She points
to the one of herself and her husband.
Is that Mom and Dad? She turns
to me, her face suddenly angry,
I don't even know where Dad is!

And I have to tell her that our dad died
when I was fifteen and she was still
in college. She folds herself over
her knees, crying bitterly.
How do I not know that?

I gather my sister in my arms, hug
her bony frame. I tell her I love her,
will always love her, no matter what.

5.

The nurses report that Nancy wanders
up and down the hallways,
all day, every day. I think she is
searching and searching and searching
for herself.

ACCESS DENIED

vacant eyes stare
at my face
>   no curiosity   no
>   recognition

It's me   Kathleen
your sister
>   she frowns
>   *Oh*   nothing more

I suggest
we walk   wrap
>   my arm around
>   her soft waist

hug her close   anchor
her listing footsteps
>   try again
>   to reminisce

but she can't retrieve
even our oldest stories

>   sorrow beats a fist
>   on that blank wall

SOLILOQUY TO THE NIGHT SKY

Oh unfathomable
universe. I depend
on your shimmer
of stars, the moon's
mother-of-pearl
luminescence,
to counter the light
vanishing
from my sister's
eyes.

I lift up
my face to all your dark
mystery, knowing
you care nothing for me.

I crave
that steady indifference,
how your cold
expanse contracts
my sorrow
down to bearable.

STILLNESS

Wooden bridge, feel my footsteps stride
across your old, musty slats.

And I will feel them give a little under my boots.

Listen to me hum some random tune as I pause
to look over your railing.

And I will eavesdrop as the creek water
gurgles its song across smooth, mossy stones.

Lead me onto the pine-needle path.

And I will follow the amble
through wildflowers, ferns, tree canopy.

Wooden bridge, this trail always circles back
to you.

I have crossed your span so many times,
we should be old friends.

But of course, we aren't.

You are part of Nature, all harmony and complete
disinterest.

And I am all runaway emotion.

Wooden bridge, I come to these woods to escape
myself, the weight of sadness.

And you afford me passage into the hush.

TENACITY

Hiking in the woods, I discover
a spindly sugar maple with gnarled
bark and a network of thick roots,
like the twisted legs of some alien
creature, curved around and down
a flat boulder, its toes dangling
in rich loam below. Such a fluke:

a seed falling into the one patch
of shallow dirt accumulated
on this giant rock, birthing a tree.
I imagine how its burrowing roots
must have hit bedrock beneath
that cradle of soil, but undeterred,
stretched up and over the boulder
towards the forest floor;
obstacle becoming support,
rock and plant finding balance.

The mature maple is stunted
but holds onto life with raw grace.

My sister would have loved
this story, once upon a time. Now
her roots are too tangled, too
choked off to follow the details.
Instead, I tell her to hang on,
to look in my eyes and see her self
anchored there.

WISHING FOR WINGS

Robins, blackbirds bathe
in the shallow end of our pond,
submerge their soft belly feathers.
Wings splash,
heads scoop water onto their backs
until they have showered
their whole bodies
and hop onto bordering rocks
to shake dry
and preen.

Such a simple ritual,
this cleansing, this release
of dust, toxins, mites
into water, air.

I think of the birds as I tug
my 80-year-old sister
onto her right side, her left,
to inch off dirty clothes, dirty diaper,
wipe her,
maneuver her again to stretch
clean clothes, fresh diaper
over her limp body.

I'm not sure her Alzheimer's-choked
brain recognizes it's me
and not a nurse. Four days inaction,
post gall bladder surgery, has robbed
strength from her arm, stomach
and leg muscles, accelerating
the inevitable. She's confined now,
a nestling.

A nurse helps me secure my sister
into a wheelchair. I transport her
to a shady patio
outside the assisted living facility.
She tilts her head back, closes
her eyes. Cardinals serenade away
our stale, institutional smell
into the fresh,
flower-scented breeze.

TRANSCENDENCE

I'm watching Amos Lee in concert on YouTube.
The camera pans the audience, lingers
on a man holding the twisted hand
of another man seat-belted
into a wheelchair, his head lolling
to one side. Their two hands bounce
in the air, keeping time with the beat.
The first man turns to the other, flashes
a conspiratorial grin; the close-up capturing
everything there is to know
about love.

LOVE HONED BY THE INSIDE JOKE

Nancy and I are doing the dishes,
a nightly chore we accept with forbearance,
flavor with our own brand of mischief.

Forbidden soapy-water fights, the wettest
of us tasked with floor mop-up. Always me,
hair and face dripping.

Conspiring to sing off key, loud and long,
gleefully anticipating the eventual effect:
exasperated parental outcry.

The two of us overcome with giggles.

DEBUSSY IN THE AFTERNOON

My sister's fingers finally master the piece.
Claire de Lune, my favorite, and the hardest one
          in her piano repertoire. Sprawled
on the couch,
                    I fold myself inside her music.

I'm the only one in the family she allows
to listen while she practices. She trusts me
          to not interrupt, to be
                         as rapt as she is.

Outside, the winter day is a monochromatic solo.
White sky intones white landscape. If I look out
          our frost-laced window long enough,
the glass
               seems to disappear. Snowflakes

become ballerinas, diamond-dusted, twirling
to Nancy's accompaniment.   A sudden
          crescendo of blackbirds surges upward
from the furrowed field
                    adjacent to our backyard.
Dark, soaring notes on a white page.

When my maestro finishes, I clap and cheer. She says,
          Oh, you like anything I play.

GUT REACTION

Hospice monitors Nancy
once a week, now. Checks
on her deterioration,
like buzzards circling
above an injured deer.

Shoo! Go away!
She's not dying.
Not my beautiful sister.

Not her.

Not yet.

LISTENING FOR THUNDER

my hands grip
metal handles
of silver wheelbarrow   steer
through open field

lightning scrolls
a skyborne warning
leave it   run to the house
danger
so specific   so clear cut

not left to be imagined
over and over

dementia gene inherited
a slow disappearance
like my sister

will I be next   cause

years of suffering
for my husband   children
grandchildren

hope   a cloudless blue sky
my pen in hand   poetry
striking the page

EDGE OF LIGHT

April dawn
animates
redbud, dogwood
bubble gum pink
frilly lace white

yellow & black
chickadees
dart, dive, alight,
feast at birdfeeder
tiny silhouettes
speckle
red ombre sky

rising sun glazes
pond water
metallic rose
goldfish flash
hint of Matisse

rush of wonder

MY SISTER SLIPS INTO MY DREAM

floats at the edge of my vision
wordless   translucent   halfway
between two worlds
one measured in closing doors
the other   in gateways
I hold my breath   eyes
unwavering

she fades   and is gone

I exhale

ELEGY FOR NANCY

too sensitive
a trait our mother never understood
considered weak
and bullied her to become
more outgoing
more confident
more popular
someone she could relate to
like me

not a daughter who loved
to read
in the solace of her room
dreamy distracted
by the stories inhabiting
her head
thick glasses too large
on her small-featured face

I felt Nancy's suffering
a constant backdrop
during family dinners
when mom badgered her
about dating or
labeled her lazy

after Dad died she lost
her defender and I had
no sway

I tried to comfort her
with silliness jokes laughs
hard to counteract
such an insidious message

maybe I did
by seeing   her
by loving   her

HUNTING FOR DAD'S GRAVE

After the burial, our mom
had declared:
That's not him anymore.
No amount of fresh flowers,
tears, or useless words
matter. Fifty years,
we've never been back.
Until today.

Stately trees drape
gold, ochre, sienna leaves
over well-tended plots.
A fountain fleur-de-lis spills
into a shallow pond.
My sister and I have only
a vague memory of where
Dad is.

Dark clouds crowd the horizon,
stir a chill wind. We zip up
our jackets, pull on gloves.
For an hour, we wander up
and down the rows reading
headstones. No sign of him.

Light rain begins to slant
across our faces. Umbrellas
up, we continue the search.
Still no luck. We are wet,
cold, close to tears, forced
to give up. Walking back
to the car, Nancy turns to me.
We'll just try another time.

We never do.

REGAINING BALANCE

yawn of early morning   Winter
all black and tan
like the Ellington fantasy
sky is chilled white   no promise
of blue today

hazelnut coffee   expanse
of silence   sadness curled up
in my lap   poetry for breakfast
prelude to writing

corner of my eye   awareness
a stirring   a warp   the way heat
shimmers above pavement
I squint into focus   a tawny deer
skimming the grass   two more
trail it   first I've seen this season

delicious joy   skips its light
across me   like a smooth stone
concentric circles   one voice
remember beauty

ACCEPTANCE

Let my sister lift up
and out
of her useless body.
Let her feel
my love rush
after her.

Let her float
in an ocean of light.
Warm, peaceful,
safe.

Let her memories
spark
within her soul,
brimming
and bright.

Let her sing
in a blur of joy,
I am whole.

HOW LONG DOES IT TAKE TO CRY?

the rainbow decides   wields
its primary colors like a barrier
against dark brooding clouds   throbs
the sky   my heart

the rainbow pierces
carefully constructed defenses
with prismed light
grief   longing   set free   like rain

slapping sideways   in a roar
across my metal roof   like trees
flinging their branches   wild
in surrender

MAGNETIC MIDNIGHT
WEDDING RECEPTION

Luminous streamers of light arc
        across the dance floor, shimmer
your skin green,
yellow,
        rare red.

The glo-sticked group
 undulates,
        whorls and sings. Their chemistry
is equal parts energy
rhythm,
        love.

Nancy turns to me, studded with joy.
        I grab her hand and coax her to dance
our own primal steps,
arms waving,
        laughter spilling out of us.

Radiance flashes her face,
        flairs in her eyes.
She is Aurora,
clearing out the dark
spaces.

ACKNOWLEDGMENTS

I wish to thank the editors of the following journals, anthologies and contests in which some of these poems first appeared, sometimes in different versions:

Coming of Age; Writing & Art by Kentucky Women Over 60, Vols 1 & 2: "No Off Ramp"; "access denied"; "Debussy in the Afternoon"

Highland Park Poetry Facebook Page, Poems of Inspiration: "Transcendence"; "Tenacity"; "Regaining Balance"

Lexington Poetry Month 2022 Anthology, Locks & Bones & Bells & Stamps & Maps: "ode to my sister"

Yearling (Winter 2023): "Magnetic Midnight"

Pegasus (Spring 2023): "Sightings"

KSPS Annual Conference Contest Winner (October 2024): "Soliloquy to the Night Sky"

East on Central (2025-2026 Edition): "Elegy for Nancy"

GRATITUDE

Many thanks to my fellow poets and mentors who encouraged and supported me during the writing of this manuscript: Marianne Peel, Shelda Hale, Linda Angelo, Laverne Zabielski, Linda Bryant, Marta Dorton, Bill Verble, Wendy Jett, Dudley Stone, Mike Wilson, Cathy Perkins, Mary Allen, Debbie Cooper, Libby Jones and Jules Unsel and the rest of the *Coming of Age* gang, and, of course, Katerina Stoykova. How lucky I am to be included in this talented group of writers! Your feedback is always invaluable to me.

A big thank you to Libby Falk Jones for taking time out of her busy schedule to not only read, but edit, my manuscript. You are a gem!

Special thanks to Marta Dorton for allowing me to use her remarkable mixed media piece, *Layers 1*, for the cover art.

My love and appreciation goes out to my husband, Charlie, for giving me the space and time I need to write, and for being my biggest fan!

ABOUT THE AUTHOR

Kathleen Gregg is the author of *Underground River of Want* (Finishing Line Press, 2021). She and her husband, Charlie, live on five acres outside Wilmore, Kentucky. When she isn't enjoying the open space and tranquility of country living, Kathleen writes and participates in two writing groups. She is an active member of the Kentucky State Poetry Society, having served as treasurer for four years. Kathleen graduated from the Author Academy program at the Carnegie Center for Literacy and Learning in Lexington, Kentucky, during which time she was mentored by Jeff Worley, Kentucky Poet Laureate (2019-2021). Her poetry has appeared in *The Louisville Review*, *Pine Mountain Sand & Gravel*, *Coming of Age Anthology Vols 1 & 2* and *Yearling*, to name a few. Her greatest desire is to inspire her children and grandchildren to live life to the fullest and not to be afraid to challenge themselves.